Dark Alley Marketing

An indie game developer's roadmap to the dark side of marketing

Steven M. Long

Dark Alley Marketing by Steven M. Long

An indie game developer's roadmap to the dark side of marketing

In association with IndieWatch.net

©2018 Steven Long

First Print Edition

ISBN: 9781981059096

To contact the author: LongWrites@gmail.com

To my wife Jennifer, for patiently allowing me to pursue my dreams.

…and also for being wicked hot.

TABLE OF CONTENTS

Thanks for checking out my little book.

I wrote this simply because I needed a handy reference for myself when working with clients and for my own projects. The marketing method explained on these pages is something that has inhabited my mind for a few years, but the mind can be a difficult place to keep organized and accessible.

So everything here is written down and permanent to use as a reference for any independent game developer that wants to make a splash and get their project noticed.

I mention many times that this is a bare-bones approach to marketing. There is so much more to know, and I'm already planning a supplement to this book, along with a marketing tool kit and many other handy nuggets.

To get access to all of my articles and tools, come be a patron of my Patreon site. It's cheap, I promise. But if you want to invest a few extra dollars, you can have me as your personal coach to answer questions, address your concerns and offer advice.

I'm also available for speaking engagements and appearances. If you're interested. Find me on Twitter @longie_long or reach out to me on IndieWatch.net.

Anyway, I hope this book is helpful. Too many indie developers have the talent and the dedication, but lack the marketing education and experience to really impact the market. So learn from my mistakes, take my advice, and remember me when you're rich!

- Steven Long

April 27, 2018

Hell, I don't know. Maybe you **don't** need this book.

Maybe you already know exactly how to get your game in front of the most possible players while spending the least possible money. Maybe. Or maybe you have plenty of money and can afford the best marketing agency to do everything for you? Maybe.

But probably not.

If you're reading this at all, it's likely *you already know you need help to market your indie game* and get it the attention it deserves.

Likewise, it's a good bet that you are thinking about doing it yourself. This is naturally going to be less effective than hiring pros, but still perfectly acceptable if you know what to do. But what I've discovered in my time working with developers is that most of them don't know the first thing about marketing. And in my opinion, they shouldn't!

A good developer will spend most of their time in their creative mind, figuring out how to bring pixels to vibrant life. You *should* be focused on perfecting the balance of your gameplay, tightening up controls, creating interesting characters, playtesting, playtesting and playtesting. You *should* be spending every available moment perfecting your characters and backstory. Developing a game is laborious to the point of being all-consuming. How could any dedicated developer possibly have time for marketing, too?

And yet if you want to succeed, *you must find a way.*

It's a tough balancing act that independent devs all face: How to find enough time to make a game that people will like, and also find enough time to make people realize it exists?

Marketing and development could easily be equal to full-time employment for an entire team, but for many indies, *there is nobody else on the team.* A one-person development company will be extremely hard-pressed to get enough eyeballs on their game. Even a small indie team will still probably not have the resources to get as much market engagement as they need to sell copies.

Good marketing is by nature either extremely expensive or extremely labor-intensive. There are no shortcuts that don't cost an arm and a leg. If you are determined to sell your game, (and you are, or you wouldn't bother reading this!) you will be working your butt to a greasy pulp.

—BUT!—

It's my intention that **this little book will help you get started marketing your indie game** and give you the bare basics you need to start putting it in front of the people you want.

How to treat this guide

Don't treat this book like an all-encompassing marketing bible. It is not. The rabbit hole goes far deeper than any of us have time to explore.

What I'm going to try to do here is give you **the tools you need** to create the framework that underlies any effective and affordable marketing strategy. Once you've charted the five Dark Alleys, you can spend money *if you choose,* in a deliberate and targeted way to develop a more robust marketing campaign and repave specific avenues to **get traffic and awareness to your game**.

Each aspect I'm going to cover could easily fill a book of its own, and occupy many more pages than this little book. (My Patreon page has more, if you haven't seen it) But for the busy development team, there probably isn't time to really dig deep. And if you spend too much time on any one of these approaches, you'll certainly neglect the others.

My method takes a balanced approach to marketing. You'll want to have all of these Dark Alley approaches in place by the time you launch. I have put them in what I think of as a chronological order, starting with your website and ending with distribution.

Who am I?

If you're going to take advice from me, you might as well know who I am.

My passion for gaming came before my earliest memories. I remember hanging out at arcades with my dad, playing Bad Dudes, Smash T.V., Ninja Turtles,

Double Dragon, Ms. Pac Man and all the classics. I remember visiting my cousin (also a self-published author) who owned a Nintendo and a good pile of games. It was always so exciting to discover what adventures awaited. I've always, always, always been hooked on games. It's my hobby, my passion and, increasingly, my career.

My passion for marketing came much later, in my senior year of college.

One of my majors (I had several) was Communications Technology—a glorified name for web design—and some of the required classes were basic marketing and advertising.

I'd never imagined there was a career field that actually engaged all my favorite strengths, but there it was. Branding, design and copywriting satisfied my need for creativity while SEO, analytics and web design scratched my more scientific itch. After too many majors and too many years in college, I had found my calling. I landed an internship and have been in the marketing industry ever since.

My clients have included big, big contracts like American Airlines, Capital One, 7-Eleven and others. But I've also worked with lots of indie devs, coaching and advising them in their marketing endeavors. I've also spent a few years working alongside Fernando at IndieWatch.net, helping (I hope) to bring his vision to life and creating a community there.

Through the years, I've noticed behavior patterns and pain points that seem to be almost universal among indie developers. I've seen where indie developers need the most help, and I've seen what they can do to be much more effective in creating market awareness and campaigning for their games. This book aims to address all of them.

It is for the big-talent, low-budget indie developer clients that I write this.

This marketing method can be operated with minimal cost and minimal effort so the developer's focus can remain on the more important aspects of development. The things we'll cover in this guide are the low-hanging fruit of marketing that will provide the highest return on your investment of time and money.

This style of marketing won't work for EA or Blizzard. Big-time marketing is necessarily expensive and inaccessible to all but the richest of hobby developers. The marketing method I'll teach in this book is tailor-made for small developers with little or no budget. The contents of this book represent the darkest backstreets and forgotten alleys of marketing. The places that triple-A developers and publishers dare not go, and indie devs can operate unimpeded. This is games marketing at its most ghetto.

Marketing's Dark Path

So…won't you join me? We can venture down the Five Dark Alleys of indie game marketing together. Why Dark Alleys? Well, think of my method as an alternative to what I call Highway Marketing.

Think about it.

Every time a corporate giant superstore gets built, they have to come in and rebuild the roads to accommodate traffic and get buyers into the store. They command that kind of power and they wield that kind of budget. **They can literally create highways to get customers in**

faster and easier and spend more money, more consistently.

Big developers work similarly. Using obscenely expensive paid advertising, they are able to create dazzling ads and leverage the biggest influencers and offer in-game content to the point they are basically bribing their customers.

Highway Marketing. Get it?

For an indie, this Highway approach is not even an option. We have to find your customers in a different way. Rather than paving a highway for them to easily follow, we have to lead them through the dark avenues of the interwebs and guide them directly where we want them to be.

Dark Alley Marketing methods will take us through already-established backstreets and across the rooftops to get **effective results with minimal budget.** My method will cover the most tried and true marketing methods available for the leanest budgets. But, **like with most backroads, taking this route will cost much more time than highway marketing**.

Also, be aware that this book and **this method is just the bare minimum for any good marketing campaign**, and when you're familiar with all five Dark Alleys, you'll be able to invest incrementally in any of them to ensure you're only paying for what you need, and aspects of your marketing that are already effective can remain as they are.

The Dark Alleys I'm going to outline in this book are what I consider the most cost-effective means of getting your game in front of the people that really matter, to make it as successful as possible, as cheaply as possible. All the methods we'll discuss are accessible to anybody willing to put in the effort and empower themselves with their own success.

Just one more thing...

I have to mention one more thing.

None of my methods, no matter how perfectly you follow them, will work if your game sucks.

Seriously hoping I don't sound too harsh here. But **before you try to sell your game to anybody,**

make sure it is pretty and playable. In my career, I've seen many devs try and fail to pass off a half-baked game as a completed masterpiece. Be real with yourself. If your marketing isn't working, it's very possible that your audience just isn't happy with the game itself. Got it? Good.

Ready to go? Okay. Welcome to the Dark Side.

Your Game as Marketing

Marketing guru Regis McKenna once said, "Marketing is everything, and everything is marketing." And he is correct. Every word spoken, every tweet shared, every post liked, every image, blog, **every single *thing*(!) about your indie game is marketing**. Even the game itself.

This means that your game—even if it's not finished yet—has a reputation to uphold. You want your potential audience—your **fan base**—to feel a certain way about your game. You want to invoke certain compulsions. You want it to be scary, funny, exciting, engaging and whatever else. But before the public can play your game, **all they know is what it looks like**.

I harp on this a lot. **The way your game looks is the number-one reason people will even take a second glance**. It needs to be pretty. And I'm not just talking about the in-game graphics. I'm saying that every aspect of your game should be polished and attractive. The menus, the dialogue boxes, player select screen and of course **the title splash screen**.

That last one is special. The title splash—the screen that pops up when a player first boots up your game—should be the masthead of your game. That is, if your game was a pirate ship, the title screen is the naked mermaid carved into the front of it. If your game was a car, the title screen would be the blaring headlights in the woods.

This is crucial! The title screen is one of the most important visual parts of your game. It sets a precedent for what's to come. If your title screen and logo are ugly, players enter your game with a pre-conceived notion that your whole game is going to be ugly and unpolished. It harms the entire **user experience** (a nice marketing term for you). If your title screen is grand and gorgeous, with an epic, swelling soundtrack to welcome the players home, they will enter your game feeling confident it is going to be mind-blowing!

The title screen is the grand culmination of the waiting, following, subscribing, crowdfunding, downloading installing and all the anticipation players feel up to the very moment they finally get to start up your game *for the first time!* So, I always recommend using your title screen concept, colors, theme and text treatment as marketing elements that should stay consistent across all the platforms you use, long before your game is actually released.

Your title screen should capture the essence of everything you've done prior to launch.

Why should anybody buy your game?

This is a serious question that you should carefully consider.

Many developers approach the market with the idea that, since they spent so many hours on their game, people should buy it. They think that people will purchase the game simply because it's there. Because it pops up in their social feed or their Steam homepage.

If you're a gamer, I have no doubt that dozens and dozens of games pass by your eyeballs every day. When you're shopping for something interesting to play, how many games do you scroll past before something looks interesting? A lot, most likely. If you approach the market with the attitude that so many other devs take, your game will be one of those. Unnoticed, unplayed, unloved. So the question again comes up.

Why *should* anybody buy your game? What makes your game stand apart from the thousands of others? What's special about it?

Finding your unique selling proposition

Marketing nerds look for what we call a **Unique selling proposition** (USP), which is a fancy-schmancy way of saying, "**the reason to buy *your* product, instead of any of the other products just like it**." You have to have a USP if you want to be successful at selling anything. Especially when competition is as fierce as it is in the world of indie gaming.

The trick to having a unique selling point is to **figure out what user need your product satisfies.** I've written about this before, and I feel like I should write about it more. A lot more. Satisfying the needs of your audience is crucial to selling and getting popular.

So when you ask yourself why anybody should buy your game, you've got to think about what your audience wants, and how you can deliver as much of *that* as you can! The easiest way to do this is to be your own audience. Most likely, whatever you want from the game is what your audience wants, too.

Depending on the genre, your audience will have different needs.

Action fans may have a need to smash through hordes of enemies, parrying and racking up combos like God of War. The intense action in God of War keeps players plugged in and constantly striving to control crowds of enemies. And since there's always one more ass to kick, it's hard to turn the game off. There are relaxed points in the game where players are challenged to do some platforming or balance-beam walking (not a fan myself) and of course very well-made cutscenes. And then it's back into the fray!

Every genre satisfies different needs for gamers. But there are nuances within that satisfaction-delivery system that should be exploited as fully as possible to make sure there is **something** your game does extremely well. It doesn't have to be the best, but if it's fun and pretty, people will still keep playing.

Some games fulfill a need for visceral violence and over-the-top mayhem. Some games provide a constant, ongoing reward system by progressing characters regularly and others reward tactical, methodical thought. Every good game you've ever played had some unique selling proposition, some *thing* it accomplished that you didn't find in bad games.

What does your game do best?

It can be tempting to say, "I want a game that constantly rewards the player AND fulfills a visceral need for violence AND rewards tactical thinking AND has a deep and satisfying story!" That may sound like the perfect game—and I can even think of a few incredible games that match this description. But for better marketing—and for your own sanity—pick **one** unique selling point.

You can do the other stuff too, but stay focused on the one thing you're sure your game can do better than any of your direct competition. If you spend too much time trying to do too many things, you will not do any of them as well.

Once you know your USP, make sure your game embodies that and market it accordingly. Let buyers know about what makes your game unique. Let them know why they **need** your game.

Spoilers of War

As your game nears completion and graphical elements are pretty much as they are going to stay, you need to start showing it off.

Many developers have a fear of giving away too much. They don't want to spoil the game. And I get that. Gamers love to be surprised. They love the feeling of discovering something for the first time. But that doesn't mean you keep your game under a tarp in the garage. Your game is its own essence! It is a massive epic of art, action and animation. Your game is an endless well of material to share with your audience. And they want to see it!

Think of all the movie trailers you've watched in your life. How many of them walk you through the entire plot, one piece at a time, highlighting the funniest jokes in the movie? Letting the soundtrack guide you through the difficult plot twists the heroes face? The epic moment of truth that always fades to black, then the title reveal? Plenty.

I've always felt a bit annoyed when a movie trailer spoils the good parts. But guess what? I still paid to see the damn movie. Your audience will, too.

Also, remember that games are different from movies in one crucial way. In a video game, the audience controls the action.

Plenty of gamers feel that a game's plot is secondary to gameplay. You might have spent years working on a backstory to fully flesh out your game world, and it's your baby. But most players consider the plot a nice bonus and won't play through a game with an intriguing storyline if the gameplay sucks.

So even if your customers know some plot elements or gameplay elements that await them, they are still in control of the action, and they're still excited to advance the plot and save the day. They aren't just reliving your game trailer or images online. They are experiencing it firsthand.

Another good justification for giving away game elements is that, rather than turning players off, it keeps them engaged longer. If your game trailer and imagery show some very big and awe-inspiring monstrous boss from near the end of the game, and that attracts players, they are going to play your game until they get to see that boss!

I'm definitely *not* suggesting you post let's plays of the entire final boss battle. But a quick glimpse of an impressive boss will impress players and get them interested in seeing more.

It is a fine line to walk, which is a recurring theme in marketing. You want to give away as much as you can, without sacrificing the value of your product.

How much you ultimately spoil in your marketing is up to you, but I always recommend that you show what is most awesome about your game. If you can artfully spare a glimpse of your massive final boss without giving away all the fun, you've found the balance.

To put it simply: **Promote the best parts of your actual game**. Cutscenes and dramatic story-based trailers are fine and all. But most players want to know what they'll actually be playing. I'll talk more about trailers later on.

Chapter Takeaways

- Your game is its own best marketing. While hype and promises of awesomeness might feel impressive to you, gamers want to know how your game will actually look and feel.

- If you're worried about spoiling the gameplay or plot elements, that's understandable. **But don't deprive potential players of the most interesting and engaging elements of your game.** Don't expect players to buy your game on faith alone. You have to show them what they're buying, even if it's just a glance.

Why you need a website

Every game needs a home. Think of your website as your game's evil lair. Your website is where your game can go take a dump, knowing its butt won't be touching other games' butt juice. No, but seriously.

Your game's website is the hub from which all the other Dark Alleys lead. This is your repository for everything you do to your game that you want anybody to see. I'll go down the list here in a minute, to let you know what exactly you ought to have on here. But to introduce the concept, I'd like to continue a bit down this frightening Dark Alley.

It's **important to purchase a domain name** and there are a number of reasons for this.

First, it will help your audience find your game. If they can remember your game's name and want to find it again, they can just add a **.com** to the end of the title. Then they have made it back to your project with minimal effort. Which reminds me of my favorite golden rule in marketing: **Customers are lazy AF**. Always assume your customers will put forth the least possible effort to find or buy your game.

Purchasing your domain name does more than make your game easy to find, it will also prove to your audience that you are serious about your project. You are invested financially in your own success. That sounds cheesy, but having a good-looking website with your own URL is a very worthwhile asset when you are going to ask people to buy something. **You want to look legitimate**.

Domain names aren't free. But you have to understand that **you aren't going to get through this without spending money**. And if you are thinking about trying to get through the development, marketing and distribution process on a zero-dollar budget, you may be riding the wrong pony. If you aren't even willing to invest the $20 it takes to reserve a web domain, why would you or your audience be convinced that you're serious at all?

And yes, I know I'm writing this book for devs with no budget. But I think **this is one investment you absolutely should make**!

When you've invested into something like a domain name, it grants a certain amount of realism to your project. It's no longer an idea or a dream. It's something that's happening. And you've put money into it. It just makes sense to reserve your URL and make an initial investment in your own effort.

Golden Rule #1

Always assume customers will do the least possible work to find or buy your game.

There are a few reasons to approach marketing with this assumption. For one thing, it's true. Nobody wants to do homework in order to spend money on something. But also, consider that your audience is on the internet: the most distracting *thing* ever invented.

Researchers claim that the human attention span online is something like 7 seconds. And when you look around at the amount of information, drama, celebrity gossip, upcoming films, news and any and every thing that could be created to fight for your attention... What was I talking about? Oh yeah, the internet is a distracting place.

Make it a habit to always tell customers exactly what you want them to do and provide a link that takes them exactly to where they can do it. In marketing we call this a "Call to Action" and it works like this:

Want to see more? Click here for more information.

See how that works? If you liked my words, you can click to pursue deeper knowledge within a second or two. If you always make it this easy for your audience to connect to your content, you will keep their attention much more consistently.

What to put on your website

I've seen all sorts of game websites from indie developers. Some of them are lavish, with clever animated buttons, videos, GIFs, images, pages and pages of back story, character illustrations and all sorts of creative stuff. And that's great. I've also seen websites with almost nothing on them but a few images. That's not great, but your website doesn't have to be over the top in order to be effective.

The truth is, you don't need a lot of stuff on your website. But there are some staples that I always look for when I'm critiquing clients' websites.

1. Home

This is where the obvious stuff should go.

- A beautiful banner for your game (something very like your title splash screen)
- The name of your game
- Some catchy phrase (Swashbuckling fun in a necrotic hamster's colon)
- Which platforms it will be on (Steam, Switch, PS5, whatever)
- Expected release date

This is pretty much the same stuff that will go in your press kit (more on that in a little bit.) You can link the other parts of your page here, too. Specifically your **blog**, where the latest news about your game will be located.

This might sound like obvious stuff. But you'd be shocked by how many developers overlook even this basic information. It's understandable, given how close developers are to their own project. Sometimes it's hard to take a few steps back and really look at your website through the eyes of your customers.

2. Subscribe

Sadly, this is something I almost never find on indie developer websites.

It can seem tough to set up a subscription email service, but tools like MailChimp make it rather easier than you might think. (And seriously, you're a developer for cryin' out loud. I'm sure you can figure it out.)

Capturing email addresses from interested visitors has many benefits that are often overlooked. Even though it can feel like slow going as you grow your email subscriber list—especially compared to the big gains you might get in your social media following—it's important to remember that **email has many times the conversion power of social media**.

Also, you may build a large following on social media, but that audience isn't really *yours*. Remember, Twitter and Facebook control their own platform. **No matter how hard you work, there is a mindless, soulless algorithm that has the final say about whether your posts are seen at all**. Somewhat recent changes to Facebook and YouTube algorithms have both left many big-time users feeling hosed.

By contrast, the emails you capture and the list you create truly *do* belong to you.

Not only will your emails be seen by almost 100% of the people you send them to (as opposed to something like 2% of tweets), but the people on your list will be receiving those emails because they have opted in. They gave you their email because the trust you send them awesome stuff.

Before your game is actually released, getting people to sign up for email is a very worthwhile focus for your marketing efforts.

By capturing email, you are engaging your audience in the long term.

It can feel like social media, your website and videos are enough to keep your audience coming back. They're not. As your social media audience grows, a small and smaller percentage of them will ever actually see your posts. The here-today-gone-tomorrow nature of social media makes it difficult to keep an audience engaged over time. But as you collect email addresses, you can repeatedly re-engage your people.

As you develop your game, you can continue to send emails illustrating recent changes to your project to reignite the excitement of your fan base.

There's a fine line here between keeping your audience informed and spamming them to death. The "less-is-more" approach is usually the best during development. But as launch approaches, you'll want to send a bit more frequently. And your captured email audience is the perfect place to tell potential players where they can get your game.

The more I learn, the more useful a good email list is proving to be. Even after your game releases, you'll have a list of people who are interested in what you're up to. You can continue to keep them informed about updates to your current release, and about whatever you're working on next. The key is to keep the momentum once you gain it and stay in touch with your audience when you have something relevant and interesting to share.

In addition to snaring potential buyers and players, an email list should be mobilized to capture influencers and promoters. Keep track of who is on your list that might also be able to influence their own audience to check out your game.

I'll talk a lot more about influencer marketing later. I think it's **one of the most important means of amplifying your fan base efficiently** without wasting a bunch of time.

3. Blog or Devlog

Maintaining a blog on your website is so simple there's no reason not to do it.

Even a monthly check-in is enough. A few paragraphs about what you and/or your team has done, what partnerships you're forging, what sprite sets you've completed, what cool features and mechanics you're perfecting. Stuff like that.

There are several reasons to do this. For one, it lets your audience know the game is alive. So many forgotten, abandoned projects are floating in the void of the internet, it's important to regularly update so anybody that finds your site can say, "oh, this thing is actually going to happen."

A second reason for having regular blog updates is arguably more important: it **engages your audience on a personal level.** Letting them know what you're up to during development gives a human aspect to your game.

While you're blogging about development, it's important to remember who your intended audience is. These are rank-and-file gamers. Other developers might buy your game, too, but it's the gaming masses you want to appeal to. A long, technical blog update about your hardware setup is fine once in a while, but what most of your audience will really want to know about is...

- **Graphics**—This is the number-one reason most gamers decide to be interested in a game or not. Sure, a game's graphics are only skin deep, and it's exciting and satisfying gameplay that will make a game successful in the long run. But **before**

anybody can buy your game, they have to notice it!

Initially, you might not have a lot of completed sprites or backgrounds to show. I suggest using a lot of concept art to show off what you intend to create and capture the imagination of your audience. Make it pretty enough for public consumption, though. Add some nice backgrounds or some color beyond what you normally would for concept art. It doesn't' have to be a lot, just enough to catch eyes and get attention.

- **Upcoming demos and betas**—If you have an audience that's following your game, remember the final goal is for them to **play it.** They might be mildly interested in the development process, but for them, playing the game is their end goal.

- **Gameplay videos and trailers**—Do you notice a pattern emerging? When you're trying to get an audience to **see** your game, **visual elements are literally the only way.** Make a new trailer every time you have some significant changes or new environments or mechanics to show off. You can't overdo it.

4. Press Kit

The press kit is so important, I've devoted an entire chapter of this book to it. For the moment though, let's just say that **your press kit deserves its own very prominent tab on your website** to make sure any visitor can find it right away. That's because the Dark Alley Marketing method involves appealing to a smaller, more targeted audience of influencers that know what to do with a press kit.

Your press kit should exist in two forms.

One should be alive and constantly evolving **on your website**. Having a version online makes it very convenient for you to update whenever you have something new to show. It also makes it easy for your influencer friends to access it from anywhere. I often find myself needing to access client work from my home computer, work computer and mobile device to track down what I need. Having your press kit online makes it easy to do that.

A second version of your press kit belongs **in a .zip file** that you can easily send to the influencers you've been adding to your email list. For those of us who blog or create other content about games, it is often more convenient to have your pictures and information saved locally to a computer.

Dark Alley Marketing treats the press kit as one of the most important pieces of marketing you can have. It grants access to your game for the influencers and players you want to see it. But the press kit is often overlooked because it's almost too simple and a lot of developers don't realize its importance. Make no mistake, having a press kit is simple and effective enough that I consider it one of the darkest of Dark Alleys of game marketing.

5. Media (Maybe)

Your press kit is your game's resume and portfolio. Put your best stuff in there, and when you make newer, better stuff, put that in, too. But make sure your press kit doesn't overwhelm viewers with too much stuff. Additional imagery and content can still live on your website, though. Keep them under a "Media" tab. You do **not** want your press kit to get overloaded. With your press kit, more is not merrier.

The media section of your site should be where your extra art, gifs, videos, concepts and whatever other sawdust you end up with, should live. For marketers that want a deep cut from your content pool, or have a clever idea for a post and need some different graphics, it's sometimes convenient to have extra content to draw from. And sometimes people are just extra-curious about your game, too.

6. Contact

Your contact information should be all over your website: on the home page, in the press kit and maybe in the header across every page for good measure.

But different folks have different preferences and many professional marketers prefer email for official correspondence. Social media is fine for casual contacts and hobby bloggers and such, but for the big-timers you want to attract, they'll probably want an email. Make it prominent in this section.

Your project email address is another smart place to spend a few bucks on a domain. A Gmail or Outlook address is fine, but YourName@YourStudio.com is marginally more professional. Not a huge deal, just a cheap hack to seem more official.

Along with your email, this is where you put your social handles, any other websites, YouTube channel and whatever other means by which you want to be found. Make yourself available!

Chapter Takeaways

- If something doesn't have a website, does it even really exist? Only kinda.

- By giving your game a place to live, you give the internet something to Google. You give your fans a place to check back regularly. You give yourself an email list of potential buyers. And you give the press and marketers access to materials they require to get the word out about your game.

- A good game website should include four to six tabs. No more than that or you're just giving visitors more ways to get distracted. My suggestion is to include the following navigation tabs:
  - Home
  - Blog
  - Press Kit
  - Contact
  - Subscribe
  - Media (only if you have enough content to justify a Media section)

Why is a press kit important?

As a developer, your press kit is worthless. What do you do with it? Nothing. It's just a place to stash a few files you've completed. But when you look at it from the perspective of the press or someone who just wants to share what you've created, that stash of files is an invaluable tool.

When bloggers, reviewers, press and whoever, decide they like your game, they want to share it with their own fans. Your press kit is the go-to place for these saints to pull things like your game's official logo, banners, GIFs, trailer, character sprites and other images. In other words, **you make it more convenient to share your game!** And you may recall that golden rule: People will put the least possible amount of work into finding, buying or sharing your game. So make it as easy as you can. For many, if it takes more than a couple of minutes to find something, they'll give up. Don't expect people to hunt for your collateral. Give it to them up front.

Having a well-made press kit also ensures that your game will be represented consistently from one review to another. Content creators won't have to pull images from elsewhere; your press kit exists to make sure everyone that writes about your game has access to the same banners and stuff. **And another golden rule in marketing is that a person must see your logo, banner or whatever, seven times** before they will remember it. So make sure your logo is being seen consistently, looking the same everywhere!

My article on IndieWatch might help put it into perspective.

…Let's imagine for a moment that you're a member of the gaming press. An IndieWatch.net writer, for example. As a writer, there are certain raw facts we need right away to determine if your game is something we can write about.

To put this into context, let's walk through a typical scenario:

1. I'm browsing the hashtag #ScreenshotSaturday on Twitter and see something I like.

2. I look at the poster's Twitter profile and scroll down to find a history of quality screenshots and insightful commentary about the project.

3. I visit the website prominently displayed on their profile.

4. I am taken directly to their website where their game press kit has its own tab and is easily accessed.

5. I now have access to all pertinent facts about the game, along with a few official banners and things I can post in any article I decide to write.

So in this scenario, the busy writer/editor/content manager (me) stops browsing because they see something they like. You've got about two minutes to completely engage me. What I find when I visit your page and press kit will determine whether I scribble down the name of your game, or if I give up looking for the info I need and click away in frustration.

As a member of the press, I am naturally drawn to your press kit. That's my kit, after all. Your press kit is your elevator pitch. It says THIS is what I'm working on, THIS is how you can get it, THIS is what it looks like, THIS is why you should be interested. In other words, **your press kit is a collection of the most basic information a visitor will need to determine whether they are interested in your game.**

You want to capture visitors' attention, but *don't* get to fancy with your press kit. A little fancy is fine, but don't let style or eye-catchingness overshadow the actual content.

How to pull it together

As for what to put in your press kit, simplicity is often the best policy. You don't want influencers getting lost in the content you've provided them.

In my mind, **there are five basic things every press kit should have**. And if you ONLY have those six things, your press kit is exactly as effective as one with more things. Perhaps more so, depending on how well organized it is. And that organization is key! If someone can't find what they're looking for, it will have a negative impact on how your game and your studio is perceived.

Items every press kit MUST HAVE

- The name of your game

Obviously. But you'd be surprised how many leave this out.

- A VERY short (1 sentence) description to push your Unique Selling Proposition—Your Unique Selling Proposition or USP is the essence of what makes your game stand out in a saturated market. Keep this short! You can talk more about the game's details later.

- A big, beautiful banner image—Put your game's "official" banner near the very top of your kit, "above the fold" as we say. Make it beautiful!

- Bullet points or facts list including

  o The platform the game will be available on (Steam, iOS, Switch, etc.)—Again, you'd be surprised how many devs leave out this VERY important stat.

o Projected release date—You can always change this later. But it's good to give folks a general idea.

o Name of studio or developer—Good media folk will want to look you up to see if you've made anything before and to refer to your studio name in their reviews. Plus you'll want to make your studio name and logo visible whenever you can.

o Website—Even for the press kit that's on your website, still include your website!

o Social media handles (Twitter, FB, Insta, YouTube)—Folks will want to follow your game if it looks good. Plus, this gives influencers a way to contact you for questions.

o Your email—Another way to make yourself reachable.

- A longer description of your game—Once you've gotten all the most basic info out of the way, you can start really telling the premise of your game, the backstory, the gameplay mechanics, its inspirations, aspirations and everything else. But please put all the other stuff first. Opening a press kit and finding a wall of text is always annoying.

...Always.

Golden Rule #2

Every marketing student learns that **an ugly brand logo that is seen often, over time, will outperform a higher-quality logo that is seen less often.**

In other words, it's probably a good idea to decide on a "brand" for your game early in the design process. Choose your colors, art style, text fonts, and overall feeling for your game wisely. That's your brand. And you want your fan base to get used to seeing it until they recognize your game instantly.

When gamers see and recognize your game, they will "feel" like it is well-known and therefore must be good. It's a mental game, and it sounds weird. But it is proven to work.

Chapter Takeaways

Your press kit should be accessible, though it really isn't meant for the masses. Your press kit is for the media, press and other influencers. So put things in there that will impress them, and that you'd like to see echoed across reviews and other coverage your game receives.

Here are the necessities of your Press Kit:

- Game title, banner and platform (Steam, PS4, Switch)
- Short, 1-sentence description
- Release date
- Studio name
- Website
- Your contact info, social handles, YouTube channel
- Beautiful images
- Your game trailers

DARK ALLEY 3 – SOCIAL MEDIA AND YOUTUBE PRESENCE

Why it's important

I would think this is a no-brainer. Social media is the biggest and cheapest way to advertise anything. And gaming communities on Twitter and Facebook are huge! YouTube is the second largest search engine in the world, and offers free unlimited hosting for all of your gameplay footage and game trailers.

If you want to be found at all—and you definitely do!— **you MUST have an established presence on social media.**

Why it's not important

Don't treat social media as your be-all end-all marketing destination.

The problem with social is that people come and go, they gain and lose interest in different projects their peers are working on. I've seen huge Twitter influencers just get bored and go AWOL for months. I've been followed by fans that just disappear. **With social media, you have no actual control over what your audience sees**.

The algorithms in Facebook, Twitter and the rest, can be tricky. And they can change at any time. So even if you're spamming your game and your info, you really have no power over whether or not people see them.

A much more powerful tool is your email list. People check their email daily, often every few hours. I check my email obsessively. Even when I'm taking a break from Twitter and YouTube (as I am now), I'm still checking my email every time I think of it. Email is far more effective, with a far higher click rate than social media. Remember that throughout this chapter.

How to get started

Don't try to overdo it.

There are a lot of social media channels and it can be tempting to try to master and maintain a strong presence on all of them. If you try to do that without a team, you will end up with a lackluster presence all around. My advice is to pick either Facebook or Twitter as your main squeeze, and plan to spend quite a bit of time on YouTube as well.

Facebook

Facebook has been taking some hard knocks lately due to their mishandling of user information and dangerously high hackability and Russian fake news. While users still flock to this platform, the future of any tech platform is uncertain. But as of this writing, Facebook is still an excellent place to get exposure for your game.

There are plenty of Facebook groups centered on sharing new and upcoming games. These can be great places to gain traction and start growing your audience. There are also plenty of Facebook groups for indie developers to just chat and hang out or reach each other for advice.

Twitter

I love Twitter. I'm pretty addicted to it (hmu @longie_long).

It's also a great place for game developers and players to hang out. The general attitude on Twitter is positive and a lot of the political divisiveness and drama is saved for Facebook. And when conversations start getting inappropriate, it is incredibly simple to mute or block other users. No problem.

With hashtags like #ScreenShotSunday and #GameDev, you can find plenty of other folks who are doing what you're doing and make friends and allies.

YouTube

As I mentioned earlier, YouTube is the second-largest search engine after Google. It's important to learn the basics of how to use it, and to keep pumping it full of your game trailers.

Another reason to love YouTube is that paying to advertise your game in-stream to other viewers is quite affordable. There is much to know and understand about making great game trailers. If there is any point in your marketing where you're even thinking of splurging, this is it. **Paying a professional to help make your game trailer is a smart investment**.

Basics for making a great trailer for your game

- **Show the pretty parts of your game**—Does this seem obvious? It should. Yet many game trailers spend minutes at a time staring at menu screens or dialogue boxes. Don't do that. Show us some graphics and/or effects.

- **Keep it short!**—For a game trailer, 90 seconds is plenty. You can make longer trailers but even in a longer trailer you'll want to keep the goooooood stuff in the first 90 seconds. Or actually the first five seconds.

- **Show variety**—If your game looks exactly the same from start to finish, then you're in trouble. We want to see different environments, different views of the game. Don't be afraid to show a few seconds of a menu or dialogue box, but keep those intermittent during dramatic or action scenes that really showcase those graphics!

- **You've got five seconds**—Most humans will click away after seven seconds if they aren't interested in something. Give yourself five seconds to capture some attention. That means you should move your studio logo to the end of your video. Make it your business to capture the audience's attention as soon as you can. Seriously. Five seconds, buster!

Reddit

Some devs have a lot of luck with Reddit. I never have. There's a strong stigma there against self-promotion. And I happen to be a serial self-promoter, so I'm generally unwelcome on Reddit.

So try by all means, but proceed with caution. If you barrel in there and start posting your own promotions, the Redditors will likely shut you down. I can't help you here. Good luck!

The Truth about Trolls

It's sad that this has to be mentioned.

While you're out there on social media, you will inevitably come into contact with the lowliest scum (and villainy) of the internet: trolls.

You might think these folks have something better to do than post negative comments about your project. It's possible they do, and they just have to make special time to rag on your game. But more likely they have no friends and spend their free time alone and looking for things to complain about.

The truth about trolls is that they are mostly harmless. You barely need to worry about them. The truth about trolls is that, **if they take the time to comment—even negatively—about what you are up to, that means that you've caught their attention**. It means there's something eye-catching enough about your project that they've decided to target it. That's good!

Remember, there's no bad publicity. Unless you count gamergate publicity but…we don't talk about that.

Just keep your nose clean, make friends and be nice to as many people as you can. The occasional troll happens to us all. Just do your best to respond in a lighthearted way that lets them know they're stupid and you're not taking their bait. If they get aggressive or offensive, feel free to turn off their comments or report them.

Whatever platform you use. You really don't have to put up with trolls, and your fans shouldn't have to either.

Chapter Takeaways

- Social media is important, but it's not everything

- Don't try to do all the social media platforms. You can't. Facebook and Twitter are great. YouTube is a wonderful place to put your trailers, gameplay footage, video devlog, and for making influencer friends.

- Make sure your trailer is incredible and attention-grabbing within 5 seconds.

- Don't feed the trolls.

Work smarter, not harder

Big-budget developers and publishers have the luxury of building their own marketing networks (highways) and using forceful paid advertising to get their games noticed. YouTube commercials, pay-per-click ads on major websites, paid features and even billboards are surefire ways to get exposure. But they come with a massive price tag that just isn't realistic for most independent developers.

The extreme alternative is to court your own audience, engaging potential buyers through your social media channels and blog posts. But let's face it: You've got a game to develop and you don't *really* have time for that.

As a professional marketer and social media enthusiast, I can tell you it's a full-time job just maintaining a consistent presence on Twitter. Trying to balance game development, a regular job, a real life and a robust social media presence will be so time consuming and labor intensive that your brain might actually explode.

So here's another instance where we can skip the highway marketing and opt for a Dark Alley approach.

Rather than trying to engage your entire audience and grow it to many thousands of interested followers, readers or whatever, pick out the biggest influencers you think will listen and take interest in your project.

Marketing is a numbers game. An old boss used to tell me, "You've gotta hear ten no's to hear a yes." And that's pretty much always true when you're trying to sell something.

Ten percent is a good, generic estimate for a conversion rate. Meaning, if you manage to get a 10% rate of impressions to engagements (10% of people that see your tweet click, expand, share or do anything to it) and 10% of those are likely to convert.

So if you manage to get your game posted in front of 10,000 people, 1,000 might actually engage with the post. And of those 1,000 people, 100 might buy it. Which is great! **But for many of us, 10,000 impressions is a lot!** And if you're balancing development time with social media time, it'll be even more difficult.

So instead of targeting the masses, try focusing on a narrower group. On your preferred social channels, including YouTube, **keep an eye out for influencers and focus on them personally, addressing them politely.** More on that in a bit.

Leveraging influencers is not easy. But it's not really all that difficult, either. Honestly, it's probably just as hard as courting your own gamer audience, but for the same amount of effort you'd expend in building your own audience, **you can multiply your exposure several times—or several hundreds of times—by getting these influencers to show your game to *their* audience.**

Influencer marketing means working smarter, not harder.

How to find influencers

Before you can pitch influencers, you've got to find them and identify them.

And you can probably expect a 10% conversion rate with them, too. For every 10 influencers you pitch, you might get one that is interested in playing and/or reviewing your game, tweeting their excitement or whatever they might do as influencers.

Naturally, this number will improve as your skills improve. But the biggest driver of this metric is how friendly and engaging you are. And that is basically impossible to measure.

Most social media platforms have an algorithm that promotes popular creators and puts their posts above many others. There is no hard and fast definition of what makes someone an influencer. The point is that **they command a large audience and their audience trusts them and shares their taste**. So if an influencer likes you, many of their fans will like you too.

Try digging through your social feeds (and don't forget about YouTube) to see what your friends like. Look for games similar to yours and see who's talking about those, too. When you find someone that is commenting and interacting about something that matches, see how many followers they have. Is it a lot? Great.

The other way to pitch your game to influencers is to email them. Search online for popular gaming blogs and YouTube channels. There are obvious big-boy sites like Kotaku, Rock Paper Shotgun and IGN, and it doesn't hurt to reach out to them, too. But if you're new, it's very unlikely that these busy sites will notice you. That's fine. If they do see you, then it's a nice bonus. But as a small indie, you're going to have to find smaller blogs and channels. Not too small though, or you're not multiplying your audience.

Keep looking and **make a list** of all the people that might be interested and who have a large audience you think would like to see your game. I recommend a list of thirty, forty or even fifty channels, social handles and websites to reach out to.

Just for funsies, see how big their combined audience is. Impressive, eh?

Just think about it. If you can target 30 influencers that have a combined audience of 300,000, that's 3,000 times the impact you would have on your own. Feeling motivated? Be careful here. Approach them with caution.

Let me tell you how.

How to pitch your game (previously published in part at IndieWatch)

When it comes to trying email influencers, there are certain bare-minimum ground rules that will help get your game beyond that initial glance.

I'm not exactly buried under game submissions, but I get enough of them that I can be choosy. And I have enough going on in my life that I can't possibly review every game that comes my way. So here are some tips to help you capture the attention of gaming influencers and avoid the void of email deletion!

Be POLITE!

The scenario below doesn't happen all the time, but often enough that I feel like it needs to be addressed. We sometimes get messages from indie developers pitching their games that read something like this:

> *"Hey, I just finished a bad ass game. Its the pinned post on my profil. DM me if u want buy it"*

Nah, I'm good. [Delete]

This message does so many things wrong. Let's break it down, piece by piece

"Hey"

Yeah, hey.

I mean, there's nothing objectively wrong with this. It's conversational. But that doesn't quite cut it with me.

I'm a stranger you'll probably never meet and you're about to ask me to do something for you. At least have the decency to find out my name or social handle or you can even call me "IndieWatch" or something. But when you just call me, "Hey", I'm assuming you quickly tapped out a message and are copy/pasting it to send to as many reviewers as you can. The last thing you want to do is seem generic, okay?

Take a moment to personally address the person you're contacting. It's polite. It shows that you are at least willing to put in some work, and it tells me you put some thought into where you're sending your game.

"I just finished a bad ass game."

If there's one thing bad asses are known for, it's not having to announce their bad-assness.

Did George Washington have to tell everyone what a bad ass president he was? Did Einstein have to tell everyone what a bad ass physicist he was? Did Muhammad Ali have to tell everyone what a bad ass he was? Well, Ali is an exception; he could get pretty braggy. But then again, you ain't exactly Muhammad Ali, are you?

We writers have a saying: Don't tell it; show it. That means you have to **demonstrate your game's bad-assness** in a tangible way that allows readers to draw their own conclusion. Confidence is good, but overconfidence will always backfire. Be humble and polite. Tell me what makes your game unique. If you just tell me it's bad ass, I won't believe you.

"Its the pinned post…"

Not everybody is going to be a stickler for **apostrophes** like me, but it's probably a good idea to try to use your best grammar. I'm a professional, after all. I'm not your buddy. Not to say that I couldn't *become* your buddy but so far, you're off to a bad start.

Also, please don't make me go to your profile and find your pinned post just to see something I never knew existed until you trolled me about it. You have to make it as easy as possible to find your game.

At this point in our contact, **I have zero investment in your project**. I have no desire to click your profile. I do not want to have to go out of my way to look at whatever game you made. And if you spent the same amount of effort on your game as you did in this message, then I really, *really* don't care.

77

Instead, try this: **Include an image of your game. The *best* image of your game!** Something that will actually interest me more than your shoddy grammar.

And include a link! That way I can just tap and go to your website or your press kit.

So, by including the image, I'm intrigued. And by including a link, even super busy (lazy) marketers like me will still have the 0.3 seconds it takes to click that link and learn more!

"my profil"

As I mentioned above: If I can't trust you to spell out entire words, how could I trust you to program an entire game that won't make me want to gouge my eyes out?

"DM me"

I'm not going to do that.

"if u want to buy it"

Sure pal.

I'm actually not sure I've ever been pitched a game quite this badly. However, I do get developers contacting me with their press kits and information but no offer of a key. And usually when I contact them, they don't respond or they tell me there aren't any keys available but I can play the demo here...

Now, look: I know I'm not PewDiePie. But even at my modest level of popularity, I don't remember the last time I paid for an indie game. Actually, I think it might have been Axiom Verge (so worth it). Unless we count Kickstarter games, but that's different.

If you want me to play it, you've got to give me a key. If I don't use the key then *oh well*. I might give it to one of my reviewer friends. But if you want to make actual money off your game, then giving away 20, 30, 50 or 100 keys isn't going to break you. It's something you need to do. If losing 100 sales WILL break you, then you aren't aiming for much success.

Giving away keys is the best way to ensure that the right people are playing your game. And by receiving a free key, influencers are more obligated to actually publish something about your game. And get this: if you give them a free key, and they don't like the game, they are far less likely to give it a bad review. Instead, they'll give it no review at all. But if they actually have to pay money for your game and it sucks, they are much more likely to review it poorly.

Think about that!

Doing it right

Here is a message that would interest me a great deal more:

--

"Hey @longie_long ! My team just finished a 16-bit style JRPG for Android. It features the classic gameplay we know you like, but with modern updates, great graphics, an engrossing story and... oh yeah, there's tons of llama poop!

Here's our press kit and we'd love to give you a key to review.

Thank you!"

--

Let's break this down.

_Hey @Longie_long !_

That's me. That's my Twitter handle. I'm already more engaged in this message.

My team just finished a...

Giving credit to those who work with you on the project shows humility and politeness. Good job!

16-bit style JRPG for Android.

Mobile games aren't usually my thing. But since I do have an Android, and you've been so friendly, I might just have to check it out.

It features the classic gameplay we know you like, but with modern updates, great graphics, an engrossing story

See how the dev isn't promising a bad ass game? He's telling me about the game and I'm drawing my own conclusion that this could in fact be a bad ass game! Plus the dev is showing that he has at least glanced at my Twitter profile and knows I'm into classic games.

and... oh yeah, there's tons of llama poop!

Say whaat!? If you didn't have my attention before (you did), you definitely have it now! This silly crap (pun intended) can really set you apart from other devs. You don't have to go this route, of course. The point is to be yourself and think outside the box.

#LlamaPoopEnthusiast

Here's our press kit and we'd love to give you a key to review.

A link to the press kit (hosted on their website). A single tap and I'm there. And I know all I have to do is reply to the email to get a download key.

And finally...

Thank you!

No, polite indie dev. Thank YOU!

If you want to pitch your indie game to influencers, you have to remember that **they owe you nothing**. Nobody is going to promote your game for you just because you made it. You must offer something special and you must pitch your game the right way.

Chapter Takeaways

- You can try to impress an army of gamers to get them to buy your game. Or you can work smarter and systematically target influencers. If you can impress a single influencer with 10,000 followers or subscribers, you're working 10,000 times more efficiently. Think about that!

- It can be difficult (extremely difficult) to get noticed by sites like Kotaku, IGN, Rock Paper Shotgun and Gamespot, but there are many, many smaller influencers that would be thrilled to check out your game and show it to their audience. Just be sure you're polite when approaching them and follow a few simple courtesies.

The last part of this method has to do with distribution: actually getting your product into the hands and hard drives of your excited and spend-happy audience. At first glance, this subject may seem more logistical or operational than marketing-oriented. But look again.

Today, **all major distributors have an algorithm to help gamers find what they're looking for**. And like every major social platform, there are ways to get an edge. Steam, Android, iOS, and most every major platform features a big store with big banners flaunting the latest and greatest games they have to offer.

This is a huge deal. This is your final and very best chance of making a sale.

Marketing at the distribution level necessarily creates a high return rate. Once your game is on a distribution platform, you're no longer cold-mailing influencers, you're no longer pestering people on social media, no longer angling to improve SEO and *hope* somebody is interested enough to actually purchase your game and become a conversion. **When gamers are browsing Steam or another distribution channel, they already have their wallets out**. They're browsing for something to buy.

Make sure that before your game gets this far in the cycle, every single thing is perfect. Your banner, your icon, your description and trailer are all going to be directly compared to your competitors. Even if you manage to make it into the big Steam banner, your product still has to look better than any of the other auto-cycling banners to get clicked.

Good luck.

Marketing's Halfway House

I'll admit that distribution is the part of this method that I know the least about. My expertise is in marketing and promotion. Distribution is a whole new beast to conquer. I've attempted many times to get distributors to share some techniques for developers to get featured, but everyone I've asked has ignored my interview requests. They are very protective of their algorithms.

I think of distributors as a kind of halfway house. Your game has been released from development, but before it can go out into the world on its own, it has to exist in a kind of limbo. Will your game get noticed, picked up and deemed ready to face the cold, hard world? Or will it stay in its halfway house to languish in obscurity?

Whether your game gets bought and played depends entirely on how you've marketed it. If nobody's heard of it, even if it looks good, they still might not choose to buy it. But if buyers see your game on Steam and think, "Oh, I've heard of that!" They are 1.5 gajillion times more likely to click on it.

After the purchase, there's the additional hurdle of Steam's 2-hour no-questions-asked refund window. You've got to make sure your game plays as good as it looks, or many of your sales will turn into refunds. It may be frustrating, but Steam has very good reason for implementing this policy, along with the listing fee they now charge. Shovelware today is less of a problem thanks to these policies.

Distribution isn't the end

In the olden days, distribution was the end of development. A team spent months or years developing a game. When it was completely done, they programmed it onto a board, sealed it in a plastic cartridge and shipped it to stores. Once the customer bought your game, you were done. Start working on the sequel.

This model is completely dead. And if you're still looking at distribution like it's the finish line, you're doing it wrong.

Early Access and Beta Releases

Today, getting a game published is relatively easy. You just submit it to whatever platform you want to use.

Approval is fairly simple (as steaming fields of bad games will attest) and once your game is out there, people are able to find it and download it. But developers today have the huge advantage of being able to update and tweak their games even after being purchased. And Steam even rewards developers for updating their games by promoting them in the "recently updated" tab of the storefront.

These days, DLC is the norm. Which is great for the longevity of many titles, but alternatively, games are routinely released with bugs and broken things for the devs to clean up later. This is terrible. And it's a big part of the reason Steam implemented their 2-hour refund policy.

Please don't release your game *officially* until it's finished.

Early Access

The only time it's okay to release an unfinished game is if you're doing so under Steam's Early Access program. Many devs make good use of Early Access and Beta releases, getting feedback from their audience and tweaking their game to make it better than ever. BUT! Don't treat Early Access as an open beta. They aren't the same. If your game sucks in Early Access, players will assume it sucks after launch, too.

There's also the fact that **the vast majority of Steam's Early Access games never have an**

official, final release. So if you're going to use Early Access, make sure you have a plan to update your game based on user feedback. And keep your audience informed. If they are unhappy about something, you should address it publicly and let them know you're doing something. But beware! **Much criticism will come from gamers whose goal is to find something wrong with everything**. You can't please everyone, but you do want to mitigate the damage that will be done to your game by negative reviews.

Mobilizing your Audience

When your game is officially available, whether via Early Access or otherwise, this is where your long journey through the other four Dark Alleys should come to fruition.

Try to be absolutely finished with any major work on your game for the last few months before release. You want to give yourself as much time as possible to stop coding, stop developing and start mobilizing your audience through your email list, every social channel, your website and your friends.

With every mention of your game's official launch, be sure to include a link where they can purchase the game. Don't expect anyone to do any hunting. Always place a link that takes them right to a page where they can make a purchase. The more times they have to click to get to your game, the more they'll get distracted or have second thoughts.

Get them to the Purchase button ASAP.

Getting HUGE on Steam

I've had a difficult time getting Steam and other distributors to provide me with concrete data. They won't release their secret formula for success any more than Coca-Cola or Google will. But it's a pretty safe bet that going viral and being featured on Steam is pretty much the same deal as getting noticed on YouTube.

It's also a fairly safe bet that Android, iOS, Playstation and other game stores have the same set up. The tricks of getting big on any platform like this are something I hope to expand much more into in my future writings (Dark Alley Marketing 2nd edition, perhaps)

Here's what I do know:

(The following is taken directly from Steam's marketing page: partner.steamgames.com/doc/marketing/visibility)

Early Access Launch Visibility

Your game or software will appear in a couple of places:

- In the "All New Releases" tab in the Early Access section.
- If any people have your title on their wishlist, they may receive an e-mail notification of its release.

Additionally, your title may appear in some other places:

- It may be recommended to specific users in various sections of the home page based on those users' preferences and tastes.
- It may appear on the "New and Trending" section in Early Access if the title is doing well.
- It can appear on 'top sellers' list on the store home page and on relevant genre and tag pages if it has achieved sales rank.

Full Release Launch Visibility

At launch, your game or software will appear in a couple of places:

- The first thing that happens is your title will start appearing in the 'New On Steam' queue and on the New on Steam page for users. This provides a baseline of views against which to measure customer interest. See Baseline Visibility below for details.
- Your title will also appear on the All New Releases list, which is linked from the Steam home page.
- If any people have your title on their wishlist, they may receive an e-mail notification of its release.

Additionally, your title may appear in some other places:

- It may be recommended to specific users in various sections of the home page based on those users' preferences and tastes.
- It may appear on the "New and Trending" section on the home page if the title is doing well. Your

title may be bumped off this list quickly if many other popular products are releasing at the same time.

- It can appear on 'top sellers' list on the store home page and on relevant genre and tag pages if it has achieved sales rank.

--

A few takeaways here.

First, you have an advantage over the competition while your game is new to Early Access.

Second, you enjoy the same boost when you launch officially.

But to me, the biggest thing here are the bonus points of visibility that are awarded to games that do particularly well. You should **make it your goal to get into the "New and Trending" and the "Top Sellers" lists**. This is obvious, of course, and will occur naturally if your game does well. And like YouTube and other search algorithms, your game will probably continue to enjoy boosted visibility for as long as it is receiving positive feedback and is selling better than your competition.

There are a few strategic points to consider here.

- Plan your releases when no other big games are coming out. Don't schedule release to coincide with Left 4 Dead 3 (I wish…) Try to ensure that your game is better, bigger and prettier than the current competition.
- Get your ducks in a row **before launch**. This means reading this book, of course, and making sure that you've explored every Dark Alley that can lead people to your game. Make sure you have an email list to let people know as soon as the game is available, blow it out on social media, announce it on your website with a link leading directly to the purchase page and…
- Reach out to your influencers **before** release.

That last one is the most important. Remember, by leveraging influencers you are working thousands of times more efficiently. You **don't have to contact 10,000 gamers if you are able to impress a single**

influencer. If possible, get copies of your game to them ahead of release so they can create teaser content, reviews and other content to hype your game and get people interested as soon as they can get their hands on it!

You only have a narrow window of opportunity to enjoy the default boost distributors give your game when it's new. So **do everything you can to exploit that time**. Get as many purchases and reviews as you can within the first week of release. Be sure to request that every influencer that has gotten a free key from you leave a review. Once you've run out of influencers to contact, then start calling your parents, your college roommates, your ex-girlfriend, and your ex-girlfriend's ex-boyfriend. And his chinchilla. And everyone else. Get those reviews fast!!

You even get a boost when you update your game.

It's true. I don't know what the exact numbers look like, but Steam says you get 5 opportunities to activate update boosts.

This is smart for Steam because it encourages devs to maintain their products. Of course, it works for you because you get more official Steam boosts. If you've got time to plan it, you can even create new art and visuals for each update to try to appeal to even more new players.

Take advantage of this little trick. Take advantage of all the little tricks!

Fourth-party distributors

Steam, Android, iOS, and all the game console markets are big, obvious and perfectly reputable distribution markets. You are almost definitely making a game for one of those. And each of them has their own internal store with pages of reviews, videos and promotions. And if you are on an indie budget, you might have a hard time getting good publicity in that massive pile of games.

Don't overlook smaller distribution sites. Companies like Kinguin, Humble Bundle, Fanatical, Indie Gala and many other discount sites have a much smaller pool of games. Kinguin even hosts Indie Valley which showcases independent developers and gives them the spotlight, while also giving them a significantly larger revenue share than bigger platforms.

As I said, my knowledge in distribution is relatively limited.

In later editions of this book I'll be better able to provide better advice. For now, just know that most of these distributors are actively looking for games like yours and it's easy to submit your creation for distribution on their site. Just like Steam, they are more likely to promote newer games. And of course, a lot of hype about your project won't hurt either.

Chapter Takeaways

- Steam has plenty of built-in boosts to expose your game. Take advantage of those to keep new players coming in!

- There are lots of smaller distribution channels with less competition that are more generous or beneficial for indie devs. And even if they're not, they still represent even more places for you to expose and sell your game.

- Make sure you are set up for success **before** your game goes live. Assume you have one week of boosted promotion on your channel. Use that time to get influencers to publish reviews and promote your game. After your game's initial launch, sales will drop dramatically if you aren't consistently selling a lot and getting good reviews.

Conclusion – What are you waiting for?

Time to turn theory into practice.

I've done my best to keep this book concise. There are tons of books out there that dive into the more technical aspects of promotion, but I've found surprisingly few that take a simple and holistic approach to the marketing cycle. Especially for indies like you!

Now that you've reached the end of this book, it's time to put this stuff into action.

Get out there and start promoting. Or if you already are promoting, look back over what you've got in place and make sure you aren't missing any components. Every Dark Alley we explored in this book is another avenue to lead customers straight to your game and buy it! And when you've got all these aspects assembled, they each work together to create a cohesive marketing campaign that will catch potential players everywhere they're likely to look.

Like I keep saying, **these are the bare bones of marketing**. These are the avenues you can exploit most easily to get your game increased exposure. But if your game is ugly, nobody will try it. And if your game is gorgeous but sucks to play, you'll get negative reviews. In other words, before you start driving traffic to your game, before you launch, even before Early Access, you'd better make sure your game is as awesome as you can make it.

When you're a big shot publisher, you can pave a highway to bring consumers right to your game. You can hire an agency to advertise or attract publishers to do it for you. You can buy billboards and expensive ads. But...

Until you've got that million-dollar budget, there are plenty of backroads: free or extremely cheap methods to attract buyers and get your game noticed. And plenty of devs before you have made a living, or gotten filthy stinking rich from developing, promoting and selling an indie game all by themselves.

So what are you waiting for? **Get out there and make some money**!

Made in United States
North Haven, CT
01 April 2023

34886467R00064